THE
DUTCH TWINS

Published @ 2017 Trieste Publishing Pty Ltd

ISBN 9780649566037

The Dutch Twins by Lucy Fitch Perkins

Edited by Trieste Publishing Pty Ltd.
 Cover @ 2017

www.triestepublishing.com

LUCY FITCH PERKINS

THE
DUTCH TWINS

Trieste

By Lucy Fitch Perkins

Geographical Series

THE DUTCH TWINS PRIMER. *Grade I.*
THE DUTCH TWINS. *Grade III.*
THE ESKIMO TWINS. *Grade II.*
THE JAPANESE TWINS. *Grade IV.*
THE IRISH TWINS. *Grade V.*
THE MEXICAN TWINS. *Grade VI.*
THE BELGIAN TWINS. *Grade VI.*
THE FRENCH TWINS. *Grade VII.*

Historical Series

THE CAVE TWINS. *Grade IV.*
THE SPARTAN TWINS. *Grades V–VI.*

Each volume is illustrated by the author

HOUGHTON MIFFLIN COMPANY
BOSTON   NEW YORK   CHICAGO

The Riverside Press
CAMBRIDGE . MASSACHUSETTS
U . S . A

To Lawrence
and other children

THE DUTCH TWINS

By Lucy Fitch Perkins

ILLUSTRATED BY THE AUTHOR

BOSTON   NEW YORK   CHICAGO

HOUGHTON MIFFLIN COMPANY

The Riverside Press Cambridge

CONTENTS

INTRODUCTION — KIT AND KAT 3

I. THE DAY THEY WENT FISHING . . . 5

II. MARKET DAY WITH FATHER 27

III. MOTHER'S DAY 55

IV. ONE SUNDAY 85

V. THE DAY THEY DROVE THE MILK CART . . 117

VI. THE DAY THEY GOT THEIR SKATES . . . 137

THE DUTCH TWINS

KIT AND KAT

This is a picture of Kit and Kat. They are Twins, and they live in Holland. Kit is the boy, and Kat is the girl.

Of course their real names are not Kit and Kat at all. Their real names are Christopher and Katrina. But you can see for yourself that such long names as that would never in the world fit such a short pair of Twins. So the Twins' Mother, Vrouw Vedder, said,

"They cannot be called Christopher and Katrina until they are four and a half feet high."

Now it takes a long time to grow four and a half feet of Boy and Girl. You know, chickens and puppies and colts and kittens always grow up much faster than twins. Kit and Kat ate a great many breakfasts and dinners and suppers, and played a great many plays, and had a great many happy days while they were growing up to their names. I will tell you about some of them.

I

THE DAY THEY WENT FISHING

I

THE DAY THEY WENT FISHING

ONE summer morning, very early, Vrouw Vedder opened the door of her little Dutch kitchen and stepped out.

She looked across the road which ran by the house, across the canal on the other side, across the level green fields that lay beyond, clear to the blue rim of the world, where the sky touches the earth. The sky was very blue; and the great, round, shining face of the sun was just peering over the tops of the trees, as she looked out.

Vrouw Vedder listened. The roosters in the barnyard were crowing, the ducks in the canal were quacking, and all the little birds in the fields were singing for joy. Vrouw Vedder hummed a slow little tune of her own, as she went back into her kitchen.

Kit and Kat were still asleep in their little cupboard bed. She gave them each a kiss. The Twins opened their eyes and sat up.

7

"O Kit and Kat," said Vrouw Vedder, "the sun is up, the birds are all awake and singing, and Grandfather is going fishing to-day. If you will hurry, you may go with him! He is coming at six o'clock; so pop out of bed and get dressed. I will put some lunch for you in the yellow basket, and you may dig worms for bait in the garden. Only be sure not to step on the young cabbages that Father planted."

Kit and Kat bounced out of bed in a minute. Their mother helped them put on their clothes and new wooden shoes. Then she gave them each a bowl of bread and milk for their breakfast. They ate it sitting on the kitchen doorstep.

This is a picture of Kit and Kat dig-
ging worms. You see they did just as their
mother said, and did not step on the young
cabbages. They sat on them, instead. But
that was an accident.

Kit dug the worms, and Kat put them
into a basket, with some earth in it to make
them feel at home.

When Grandfather came, he brought a
large fishing-rod for himself and two little
ones for the Twins. There was a little hook
on the end of each line.

Vrouw Vedder kissed Kit and Kat good-
bye.

"Mind Grandfather, and don't fall into
the water," she said.

Grandfather and the Twins started off together down the long road beside the canal.

The house where the Twins lived was right beside the canal. Their father was a gardener, and his beautiful rows of cabbages and beets and onions stretched in long lines across the level fields by the roadside.

Grandfather lived in a large town, a little way beyond the farm where the Twins lived. He did not often have a holiday, because he carried milk to the doors of the people in the town, every morning early. Sometime I will tell you how he did it; but I must not tell you now, because if I do, I can't tell you about their going fishing.

This morning, Grandfather carried his rod and the lunch-basket. Kit and Kat carried the basket of worms between them, and their rods over their shoulders, and they were all three very happy.

They walked along ever so far, beside the canal. Then they turned to the left and walked along a path that ran from the canal across the green fields to what looked like a hill.

But it was n't a hill at all, really, because there are n't any hills in Holland. It was a long, long wall of earth, very high — oh, as high as a house, or even higher! And it had sloping sides.

There is such a wall of earth all around the country of Holland, where the Twins live. There has to be a wall, because the sea is higher than the land. If there were no walls to shut out the sea, the whole country would be covered with water; and if that were so, then there would n't be any Holland, or any Holland Twins, or any story. So you see it was very lucky for the Twins that the wall was there. They called it a dyke.

Grandfather and Kit and Kat climbed the dyke. When they reached the top, they sat down a few minutes to rest and look at the great blue sea. Grandfather sat in the middle, with Kit on one side, and Kat on the

other; and the basket of worms and the basket of lunch were there, too.

They saw a great ship sail slowly by, making a cloud of smoke.

"Where do the ships go, Grandfather?" asked Kit.

"To America, and England, and China, and all over the world," said Grandfather.

"Why?" asked Kat. Kat almost always said "Why?" and when she did n't, Kit did.

"To take flax and linen from the mills

of Holland to make dresses for little girls in other countries," said Grandfather.

" Is that all ? " asked Kit.

" They take cheese and herring, bulbs and butter, and lots of other things besides, and bring back to us wheat and meat and all sorts of good things from the lands across the sea."

" I think I 'll be a sea captain when I 'm big," said Kit.

" So will I," said Kat.

" Girls can't," said Kit.

But Grandfather shook his head and said:

" You can't tell what a girl may be by the time she 's four feet and a half high and is called Katrina. There 's no telling what girls will do anyway. But, children, if we stay here we shall not catch any fish."

So they went down the other side of the dyke and out onto a little pier that ran from the sandy beach into the water.

Grandfather showed them how to bait their hooks. Kit baited Kat's for her, because Kat said it made her all wriggly in-

side to do it. She did not like it. Neither did the worm!

They all sat down on the end of the pier. Grandfather sat on the very end and let his wooden shoes hang down over the water; but he made Kit and Kat sit with their feet stuck straight out in front of them, so they just reached to the edge, — "So you can't fall in," said Grandfather.

They dropped their hooks into the water and sat very still, waiting for a bite. The sun climbed higher and higher in the sky, and it grew hotter and hotter on the pier. The flies tickled Kat's nose and made her sneeze.

"Keep still, can't you?" said Kit crossly. "You'll scare the fish. Girls don't know how to fish, anyway."

Pretty soon Kat felt a queer little jerk on her line. She was perfectly sure she did.

Kat squealed and jerked her rod. She jerked it so hard that one foot flew right up in the air, and one of her new wooden shoes went — splash — right into the water!

But that wasn't the worst of it! Before

16

you could say Jack Robinson, Kat's hook
flew around and caught in Kit's clothes and
pricked him.

Kit jumped and said "Ow!" And then
— no one could ever tell how it happened
— there was Kit in the water, too, splash-
ing like a young whale, with Kat's hook
still holding fast to his clothes in the back!

Grandfather jumped then, too, you may
be sure. He caught hold of Kat's rod and

pulled hard and called out, "Steady there, steady!"

And in one minute there was Kit in the shallow water beside the pier, puffing and blowing like a grampus!

Grandfather reached down and pulled him up.

When Kit was safely on the pier, Kat threw her arms around his neck, though the water was running down in streams from his hair and eyes and ears.

"O Kit," she said, "I truly thought it was a fish on my line when I jumped!"

"Just like a g-g-girl," said Kit. "They don't know how to f-f-fish." You see his teeth were chattering, because the water was cold.

"Well, anyway," said Kat, "I caught more than you did. I caught you!"

Then Kat thought of something else She shook her finger at Kit.

"O Kit," she said, "Mother told you *not* to fall into the water!"

"'T-t-twas all your fault," roared Kit. "Y-y-you began it! Anyway, where is your new wooden shoe?"

"Where are both of yours?" screamed Kat.

Sure enough, where were they? No one had thought about shoes, because they were thinking so hard about Kit.

They ran to the end of the pier and looked. There was Kat's shoe sailing away toward America like a little boat! Kit's were still bobbing about in the water near the pier.

"Oh! Oh! Oh!" shrieked Kat; but the tide was going out and carrying her shoe farther away every minute. They could not get it; but Grandfather reached down with his rod and fished out both of Kit's shoes. Then Kat took off her other one and her stockings, and they all three went back to the beach.

Grandfather and Kat covered Kit up with

sand to keep him warm while his clothes
were drying. Then Grandfather stuck the
Twins' fish-poles up in the sand and tied
the lines together for a clothes-line, and
hung Kit's clothes up on it, and Kat put
their three wooden shoes in a row beside
Kit.

Then they ate their luncheon of bread
and butter, cheese, and milk, with some rad-
ishes from Father's garden. It tasted very
good, even if it was sandy. After lunch
Grandfather said,

"It will never do to go home without any fish at all."

So by and by he went back to the pier and caught one while the Twins played in the sand. He put it in the lunch-basket to carry home.

Kat brought shells and pebbles to Kit, because he had to stay covered up in the sand, and Kit built a play dyke all around himself with them, and Kat dug a canal outside the dyke. Then she made sand-pies in clam-shells and set them in a row in the sun to bake.

They played until the shadow of the dyke grew very long across the sandy beach, and then Grandfather said it was time to go home.

He helped Kit dress, but Kit's clothes were still a little wet in the thick parts. And Kat had to go barefooted and carry her one wooden shoe.

They climbed the dyke and crossed the fields, and walked along the road by the canal. The road shone, like a strip of yellow ribbon across the green field. They walked quite slowly, for they were tired and sleepy.

By and by Kit said, "I see our house"; and Kat said, "I see Mother at the gate."

Grandfather gave the fish he caught to Kit and Kat, and Vrouw Vedder cooked it for their supper; and though it was not a very big fish, they all had some.

Grandfather must have told Vrouw Vedder something about what had happened; for that night, when she put Kit to bed, she felt of his clothes carefully — but she did n't say a word about their being damp. And she said to Kat: "To-morrow we will see the shoemaker and have him make you another shoe."

Then Kit and Kat hugged her and said good-night, and popped off to sleep before you could wink your eyes.

II

MARKET DAY WITH FATHER

II

MARKET DAY WITH FATHER

ONE afternoon Kit and Kat were playing around the kitchen doorstep, while their Mother sat on a bench by the door, peeling some onions for supper. It was not yet supper-time, but Vrouw Vedder was always ahead of the clock with the work.

Kit and Kat had a pan of water and were teaching their ducklings to swim. They each had one little fat duckling of their very own. The ducklings squawked when Kit lifted them over the edge of the pan into the water.

"Don't do that, Kit," said Kat. "The ducklings don't like it. You did n't like it when *you* fell into the water, did you?"

"But I 'm not a duck," said Kit.

"Well, anyway, they 're tired and want to go to their mother," said Kat. "Let 's do something else! I'll tell you what! Let's go out to the garden and help Father get the boat loaded for market."

"All right," said Kit. "May we, Mother?"

"Yes," said Vrouw Vedder; "and you may ask Father if he will take you to market with him to-morrow if it's fair. Tell him I said you could ask."

"Oh, goody, goody!" said Kit and Kat, both at once; and they ran as fast as their wooden shoes would take them out into the garden.

They found their father cutting cabbages and gathering them into piles. He was stopping to light his pipe, when they reached him.

"O Father!" said Kit and Kat both together. "May we go on the boat to market with you to-morrow morning? Mother said we might ask!"

Father Vedder blew two puffs from his pipe without answering.

"We'll help you load the boat," said Kit.

"Yes," said Kat, "I can carry a cab·
bage."

"I can carry two," said Kit. "We'll both
be good," said Kat.

"Very well," said Father, at last. "We'll
see how you work! And to-morrow morning, if it's fair, I'll see! But you must go to
bed early to-night, because you'll have to
get up very early in the morning, if you go

with me! Now you each take a cabbage and run along."

Father Vedder went back to his work.

Kit and Kat ran to the cabbage-pile. Kat took one, and Kit took two — just to show that he could.

"When Father says 'I'll see,' he always means 'yes,'" Kat said to Kit.

Perhaps it seems queer to you that they should go to market in a boat, but it did n't seem queer at all to the Twins.

You see, in Holland there are a great many canals. They cross the fields like roadways of water, and that is what they really are. Little canals open into big ones, and big ones go clear to the sea.

It is very easy for farmers to load their vegetables for market right on a boat. They can pull the boat out into the big canal, and then away they go to sell their produce in the town.

The canals flow through the towns, too, and make water streets, where boats go up and down as carriages go here.

33

The Twins and their father worked like beavers, washing the vegetables and packing them in baskets, until their good old boat was filled with cabbages and onions and beets and carrots and all sorts of good things to eat.

By that time it was nearly dark, and they were all three very hungry; so they went home.

They found that Mother Vedder had made
buttermilk porridge for supper. The Twins
loved buttermilk porridge. They each ate
three bowls of it, and then their mother put
them to bed.

This is a picture of the bed! It opened

like a cupboard right into the kitchen, and it was like going to bed on a shelf in the pantry.

The very next thing the Twins knew, it was morning, and there was Vrouw Vedder calling to them.

"It's market day, and the sun is almost up. Come Kit and Kat, if you want to go with Father," she said.

The Twins bounced out like two rubber balls. They ate some breakfast and then ran to the boat.

Father was there before them. He helped them into the boat and put them both on one seat, and told them to sit still. Then he got in and took the pole and pushed off.

Vrouw Vedder stood on the canal bank to see them pass.

"Be good children; mind Father, and don't get lost," she called after them.

Kit and Kat were very busy all the way to town, looking at the things to be seen on each side of the canal.

It was so early in the morning that the

grass was all shiny with dew. Black and white cows were eating the rich green grass, and a few laborers were already in the fields.

They passed little groups of farm buildings, their red-tiled roofs shining in the morning sun; and the windmills threw long, long shadows across the fields.

The blue blossoms of the flax nodded to them from the canal bank; and once they saw a stork fly over a mossy green roof, to her nest on the chimney, with a frog in her mouth.

They went under bridges and by little canals that opened into the main canal. They passed so close to some of the houses that Kit and Kat could see the white curtains blowing in the windows, and the pots of red geraniums standing on the sill. In one house the family waved their hands to Kit and Kat from the breakfast table, and a little farther on they passed a woman who was washing clothes in the canal. Other boats filled with vegetables and flowers of all colors passed them. And they were going to market too. Only no other boat had twins in it.

"Good day, neighbor Vedder," one man called out. "Are you taking a pair of fat pigs to market?"

By and by they came to the town. There were a great many boats in the canal here, and people calling back and forth to each other from them.

Kit and Kat saw a boat that the Captain's family lived in. It was like a floating house.

The Twins thought it must be grand to live on a boat like that, just going about from town to town, seeing new sights every day.

"We should never have to go to school at all," said Kit.

They wished their own boat were big enough to move about in; but Father told them they must sit very, very still all the time.

There were houses on each side of the canal, in the town, and people were clattering along over the pavement in their wooden shoes.

The market-place was an open square in the middle of the town. It had little booths and stalls all about it. The farmers brought their fresh vegetables and flowers, or whatever they had to sell, into these stalls, and then sat there waiting for customers.

Kit and Kat helped their father to unload the boat. Then they sat down on a box, and Father gave them each some bread and cheese to eat; for they were hungry again. They put the cheese between slices of bread and took bites, while they looked about.

Soon there were a good many people in the square. Most of them were women with market baskets on their arms. They went to the different stalls to see what they would buy for dinner.

A large woman with a big basket on her arm came along to the stall where Kit and Kat were sitting.

"Bless my heart!" she said. "Are you twins?"

"Yes, Ma'am," said Kit and Kat. And Kat said, "We're five years old."

"O my soul!" said the large woman. "So you are! What are your names?"

"Christopher and Katrina, but they call us Kit and Kat for short." It was Kat who said this. And Kit said,

"When we are four feet and a half high, we are going to be called Christopher and Katrina."

"Well, well, well!" said the large woman. "So you are! Now my name is Vrouw Van der Kloot. Are you helping Father?"

"Yes," said the Twins. "We're going to help him sell things."

"Then you may sell me a cabbage and ten onions," said Vrouw Van der Kloot.

Father Vedder's eyes twinkled, and he smoked his pipe. Kit got a cabbage for the Vrouw.

"You can get the ten onions," he said to Kat. You see, really Kit could n't count ten and be sure of it. So he asked Kat to do it.

Kat was n't afraid. She took out a little pile of onions in a measure, and said to Vrouw Van der Kloot,

"Is that ten?"

Then Vrouw Van der Kloot counted them with Kat, very carefully. There were eleven, and so she gave back one. Then she gave Kat the money for the onions, and Kit the money for the cabbage.

Father Vedder said,

"Now Kit and Kat, by and by, when you get hungry again, you can go over to Vrouw Van der Kloot's stall and buy something from her. She keeps the sweetie shop."

"Oh! Oh!" cried Kit and Kat. "We're hungry yet! Can't we go now?"

"No, not now," said Father. "We must do some work first."

The Twins helped Father Vedder a long
time. They learned to count ten and to do
several other things. Then their father gave
them the money for the cabbage and the ten
onions they had sold to Vrouw Van der
Kloot, and said,

"You may walk around the market and
look in all the stalls, and buy the thing you
like best that costs just two cents. Then
come back here to me."

Kit and Kat set forth on their travels, to see the world. They each held the money tightly shut in one hand, and with the other hand they held on to each other.

"The world is very large," said Kit and Kat.

They saw all sorts of strange things in the market. There were tables piled high with flowers. There was a stall full of birds in cages, singing away with all their might. One cage had five little birds in it, sitting in a row.

"O Kit," cried Kat, "let's buy the birds!"

They asked the woman if the birds cost two cents, and she said,

"No, my angels; they cost fifty cents."

You see, now that the Twins could count ten, they knew they couldn't get the birds for two cents when they cost fifty. So they went to the next place.

There, there were chickens and ducks for sale. But the Twins had plenty of those at home. There were stalls and stalls of veg--

etables just like Father's, and there were booths where meat and fish and wood and peat were sold. But the Twins could n't find anything they wanted that cost exactly two cents.

At last, what should they see but Vrouw Van der Kloot's fat face smiling at them from a stall just full of cakes and cookies and bread, and chocolate, and honey cakes, and goodies of all kinds.

The Twins held up their money.

There on the counter was a whole row of St. Nicholas dolls with currant eyes, and they knew at once that there was nothing else in all the market they should like so much!

"Do these cost two cents apiece, dear Vrouw Van der Kloot?" asked Kat.

"No," said Vrouw Van der Kloot; "they cost one cent apiece."

The Twins were discouraged.

"I don't believe there's a single thing in this whole market that costs just two cents," said Kat.

"Keep still!" said Kit. "Let me think."

They sat down on the curb. Kat kept still, and Kit took hold of his head with both hands and thought hard. He thought so hard that he scowled all over his forehead!

"I tell you what it is, Kat," he said at last. "If those St. Nicholas dolls cost one cent apiece, I *think* we could get two of them for two cents."

"O Kit," said Kat, "how splendidly you can think! Does it hurt you much? Let's ask Vrouw Van der Kloot."

They went back to the good Vrouw, who was selling some coffee bread to a woman with a basket.

"O Vrouw Van der Kloot," said Kat, "Kit says that if those St. Nicholas dolls cost one cent apiece, he *thinks* we could get two for two cents. Do you think so?"

"Of course you can," said Vrouw Van der Kloot; and she winked at the lady with the bread.

"But you 've got two cents, and I 've got two," said Kat to Kit. "If you should get two St. Nicholas dolls, why, I should have my two cents left; should n't I? Oh! dear, it won't come out right anyway!"

"Let me think some more," said Kit; and when he had thought some more, he said,

"I 'll tell you what let 's! You get two with your two cents, and I 'll get two with mine! And I 'll give my other one to Mother and you can give your other one to Father!"

"That's just what we'll do," said Kat.

They went back to Vrouw Van der Kloot.

"We'll take *four* dolls," said Kat.

"Well, well, well!" said the Vrouw. "So you've figured it all out, have you?" And she counted out the dolls — "One for Kit, and one for Kat, and one for Father, and one for Mother, and an extra one for good measure!"

"O Kit, she's given us one more!" said Kat. "Let's eat it right now! Thank you, dear Vrouw Van der Kloot."

So they ate up the one more then and there, beginning with the feet. Kit bit one off, and Kat bit the other; and they took turns until the St. Nicholas doll was all gone.

Then they took the four others, said good-bye to the good Vrouw, and went back to Father's stall. They found that Father had sold all his things and was ready to go home.

They carried their empty baskets back

to the boat, and soon were on their way
home. The Twins sat on one seat, holding
tight to their dolls, which were growing
rather sticky.

The boat was so light that they went
home from market much more quickly than
they had come, and it did not seem long
before they saw their own house. There it
was, with its mossy roof half hidden among
the trees, and Vrouw Vedder waiting for
them at the gate.

Dinner was all ready, and the Twins set the four St. Nicholas dolls in a row, in the middle of the table.

"There's one for Father, and one for Mother, and one for Kat, and one for me," said Kit.

"O Mother," said Kat, "Kit can think! He thought just how many dolls he could buy when they were one for one cent! Isn't it fine that he can do that?"

"You've learned a great deal at the market," said Vrouw Vedder. But Kit didn't say a word. He just looked proud and pleased and put his hands in his pockets.

"By and by, when you are four and a half feet high and are called Christopher, you can go with Father every time," said Vrouw Vedder.

"I can think a little bit, too," said Kat. "Can't I go?"

"No," said Vrouw Vedder. "Girls shouldn't think much. It isn't good for them. Leave thinking to the men. You can stay at home and help me."

III
MOTHER'S DAY

III

MOTHER'S DAY

"YESTERDAY was a very long day," said Vrouw Vedder on the morning after Market Day. "You were gone such a long time."

Kat gave her mother a great hug.

"We'll stay with you all day to-day, Mother," she said. "Won't we, Kit?"

"Yes," said Kit; and he hugged her too.

"And we'll help you just as much as we helped Father yesterday. Won't we, Kit?"

"More," said Kit.

"I shouldn't wonder!" said Father.

"I shall be glad of help," said Vrouw Vedder, "because Grandma is coming, and I want everything to be very clean and tidy when she comes. I'm going first to the pasture to milk the cow. You can go with me and keep the flies away. That will be a great help."

Vrouw Vedder put a yoke across her shoulders, with hooks hanging from each end of it. Then she hung a large pail on one of the hooks, and a brass milk can on the other. She gave Kat a little pail to carry, and Kit took some switches from the willow tree in the yard, with which to drive away the flies. Then they all three started down the road to the pasture.

Pretty soon they came to a little bridge over the canal, which they had to cross.

" Oh, dear," said Kat, looking down at the water, "I'm scared!" You see, there was no railing at all to take hold of, and the bridge was quite narrow.

"Ho! 'Fraidy cat!" said Kit. "I'll go first and show you how."

"And I'll walk behind you," said Vrouw Vedder.

Kat walked very slowly and held on hard

to her pail, and so she got over the bridge
safely.

"When I'm four feet and a half high,
I'm going to jump over the canal on a jump-
ing pole," said Kit.

"O how brave you are!" said Kat. "I
should be scared. And besides I'm afraid I
should drop my shoes in the water."

"Well, of course," said Kit, "boys can do a great many things that girls can't do."

When they reached the pasture, there was Mevrouw Holstein waiting for them. Mevrouw Holstein was the cow's name. Kit and Kat named her.

Vrouw Vedder tucked up her skirts — and that was quite a task, for she wore a great many of them — and sat down on a little stool. Kit and Kat stood beside her and waved their willow wands and said "Shoo!" to the flies; and Vrouw Vedder began to milk.

Mevrouw Holstein had eaten so much of the green meadow grass that Vrouw Vedder filled both the big pail and the brass can, and the little pail too, with rich milk.

"I shall have milk enough to make butter and cheese," said Vrouw Vedder. "There are no cows like our Dutch cows in all the world, I believe."

"O Mother, are you going to churn to-day?" asked Kat.

"Yes," said the Vrouw, "I have cream enough at home to make a good roll of butter, and you may help me if you will be very careful and work steadily."

"I will be very steady," said Kat. "I'm big enough now to learn."

"All Dutch girls must know how to make good butter and cheese," said Vrouw Vedder.

"And boys can drink the buttermilk," said Kit.

"I'll drink some too," said Kat.

"There'll be plenty for both," said their mother.

When she had finished milking, Vrouw Vedder shook out her skirts, put the yoke across her shoulders again and lifted the large pail of milk. She hung it on one of the hooks and the brass milk can on the other. Kat took the small pail, and they started back home. The milk was quite heavy, so they walked slowly.

They had crossed the bridge and were just turning down the road, when what should

they see but their old goose and gander walking along the road, followed by six little goslings!

"O Mother, Mother," screamed Kat; "there is the old goose that we haven't seen for so long! She has stolen her nest and hatched out six little geese all her own! They are taking them to the canal to swim."

"Quick, Kit, quick!" said Vrouw Vedder. "Don't let them go into the canal! We must drive them home."

Kit ran boldly forward in front of them, and Kat ran too. She spilled some of the milk; but she was in such a hurry that she never knew it until afterwards, when she found some in her wooden shoes!

"K-s-s-s!" said the old goose; and she
ran straight for the Twins with her mouth
open and her wings spread! The old gander
ran at them too. I can't begin to tell you
how scared Kat was then! She stood right
still and screamed.

Kit was scared too; but he stood by Kat, like a brave boy, and shook his willow switches at the geese, and shouted "Shoo! Shoo!" just as he did at the flies.

Vrouw Vedder set her pails down in the road and came up behind, flapping her apron. Then the old goose and the gander and all the little goslings started slowly along the road for home, saying cross words in Goose talk all the way!

Father Vedder was working in the garden, when the procession came down the road. First came the geese, looking very

indignant, and the goslings. Then came Kit with the leaves all whipped off his willow switches. Then came Kat with her pail; and, last of all, Vrouw Vedder and the milk!

When the new family of geese had been taken care of, and the fresh milk had been put away to cool, Vrouw Vedder got out her churn and scalded it well. Then she put in her cream, and put the cover down over the handle of the dasher.

" Now, Kit and Kat, you may take turns," she said, "and see which one of you can bring the butter, but be sure you work the dasher very evenly or the butter will not be good."

" Me first! " said Kat, and she began. Kit sat on a little stool and watched for the butter.

Kat worked the dasher up and down, up and down. The cream splashed and splashed inside the churn, and a little white ring of spatters came up around the dasher.

Kat worked until her arms ached.

"Now it's my turn," said Kit. Then he took the dasher, and the cream splashed and splashed for quite a long time; but still the butter did not come.

"Ho!" said Kat. "You're nothing but a boy. Of course you don't know how to churn. Let me try." And she took her turn.

Dash! Splash! Splash, dash! She worked away; and very soon, around the dasher, there was a ring of little specks of butter.

"Come, butter, come! Come, butter, come!
Some for a honey cake, and some for a bun,"

she sang in time to the dasher; and truly, when Vrouw Vedder opened the churn, there was a large cake of yellow butter!

Vrouw Vedder took out the butter and worked it into a nice roll. Then she gave each of the Twins a cup of buttermilk to drink.

While the Twins drank the buttermilk, their mother washed the churn and put it away. When she was all through, it was still quite early in the morning, because they had gotten up with the sun.

"Now we must clean the house," she said.

So she got out her scrubbing-brushes, and mops, and pails, and dusters, and began.

First she shook out the pillows of the best bed, that nobody ever slept in, and pushed back the curtains so that the em-

broidered coverlet could be seen. Then she put the other beds in order and drew the curtains in front of them.

She dusted the linen press and left it open just a little, so that her beautiful rolls of white linen, tied with ribbons, would show. Kat dusted the chairs, and Kit car-

ried the big brass jugs outside the kitchen
door to be polished.

Then they all three rubbed and scoured
and polished them until they shone like the
sun.

"Now it is time to cook the dinner," said
Vrouw Vedder. "We will have pork and
potatoes and some cabbage. Kit, run to the
garden and bring a cabbage; and Kat, you
may get the fire ready to cook it, when Kit
brings it in."

Kat went to the stove — but it was such a funny stove! It wasn't a stove at all, really.

There was a sort of table built up against the chimney. It was all covered with pretty blue tiles, with pictures of boats on them. Over this table, there was a shelf, like a mantel shelf. There were plates on it, and from the bottom of the shelf hung some chains with hooks on them. The coals were right out on the little table.

Kat took the bellows and — puff, puff, puff! — made the coals burn brighter. She peeped in the kettle to see that there was water in it. Then she put some more charcoal on the fire.

Kit brought in the cabbage, and Vrouw Vedder cut it up and put it into the pot of water hanging over the fire. She put the pork and potatoes in too.

In a little while the pot was bubbling away merrily; and Father Vedder, who was in the garden, sniffed the air and said,

"I know what we are going to have for dinner."

While the pot boiled, Vrouw Vedder scrubbed the floor and wiped the window.

Then she took her brooms and scrubbing-brush outside.

She scrubbed the door and the outside of the house. She scrubbed the little pig with soap. The little pig squealed, because she got some soap in its eyes. She scrubbed the steps—and even the trunk of the poplar tree in the yard! She scrubbed everything in sight, except Father Vedder and the Twins! By and by she came to the door and called,

"Come to dinner! Only be sure to leave your wooden shoes outside, when you come into my clean kitchen."

Here are the shoes, just as they left them, all in a row. And as it was Saturday, the shoes were scrubbed too, that night.

When the dinner was cleared away, Vrouw Vedder said to the Twins,

"It is almost time for Grandmother to come. Let's walk out to meet her."

They walked clear to the edge of the town before they saw her coming. They walked on top of the dyke, so they could look right down into the street, and see all the houses in a row. Grandmother was coming up the street with a basket on her arm.

74

"What do you think is in that basket?"
Vrouw Vedder asked the Twins.

"Honey cake!" said Kit; and Kat said,
"Candy!"

And Kit and Kat were both right. There
was a large honey cake and anise candies,
and some currant buns besides!

Grandmother let them peep in and see.
They were very polite and did not ask for any
—Vrouw Vedder was proud of the Twins'
good manners. Grandmother said,

"This afternoon, when we have tea, you shall have some."

"I'm glad I ate such a lot of dinner," said Kit to Kat, as they walked along; "or else I'd just have to have a bun this minute!"

"Yes," said Kat, "it's much easier to be polite when you aren't hungry."

When they got home, Kit and Kat took their Grandmother to see the new goslings, and to see the ducklings too. And Vrouw Vedder showed her the butter that Kit and Kat had helped to churn; and Grandmother said,

"My, my! What helpers they are getting to be!" Then she said, "How clean the house is!" and then, "How the brasses shine!"

"Yes," said Vrouw Vedder; "the Twins helped me make everything clean and tidy to show to you."

"I guess it's time for honey cake," said Grandmother.

Then Vrouw Vedder stirred up the fire again and boiled the kettle and made tea. She took down her best china cups and put them out on the round table.

Then Grandmother opened her basket
and took out the honey cake and buns and
the candy; and Vrouw Vedder brought out
her fresh butter.

"I can't stay polite much longer," said
Kit to Kat.

Grandmother gave them each a thin slice
of honey cake and a bun; and Vrouw Vedder spread some of the butter on the buns
—and oh, how good they were!

77

> " Some for a honey cake,
>   And some for a bun,"

sang Kat. It did n't take the Twins long to
finish them.

When they had drunk their tea, Grandmother brought out her knitting, and Mother
Vedder began to spin.

"How many rolls of linen have you ready
for Kat when she marries?" Grandmother
asked.

"I try to make at least one roll each year;
so she has four now and I am working on
the fifth one," said Vrouw Vedder. "She
shall be as well-to-do as any farmer's daughter near here, when she marries. See, this
is the last one," and Vrouw Vedder took
from the press a roll of beautiful white linen
tied with blue ribbons.

"Is that for me, Mother?" asked Kat.

"Yes," said Vrouw Vedder. "When you
marry, we shall have a fine press full of linen
for you."

"Is n't Kit going to have some too?"
asked Kat.

Grandmother laughed.

"The mother of the little girl who will some day marry Kit, is working now on her linen, no doubt; so Kit won't need any of yours."

The Twins looked very solemn and went out into the yard. They sat down on the bench by the kitchen door together. Then Kat said,

"Kit, do you s'pose we 've *got* to be married?"

"It looks like it," said Kit.

Things seemed very dark indeed to the Twins.

"Well," said Kat, "I just tell you I 'm not going to do it. I 'm going to stay at home with Mother and Father, and you and the ducks and everything!"

"What will they do with the linen then?" said Kit. "I guess you 'll *have* to be married."

Kat began to cry.

"I 'll just go and ask Mother," she said.

"I 'll go with you," said Kit. "I don't want to any more than you do."

So the Twins got down from the bench and went into the kitchen where Grandmother and Vrouw Vedder were.

Their mother was spinning flax to make linen thread.

"Mother," said the Twins, "will you please excuse us from being married."

"O my soul!" said Vrouw Vedder. She seemed surprised.

"We don't want to at all," said Kat.

"We'd rather stay with you."

"You shan't be married until after you are four feet and a half high and are called Christopher and Katrina anyway," said Vrouw Vedder. "I promise you that."

The Twins were much relieved. They went out and fed their ducklings. They felt so much better that they gave them an extra

handful of grain, and they carried a bun to
Father Vedder, who was hoeing in the far-
thest corner of the garden. He ate it, lean-
ing on his hoe.

When they went back to the house, it
was late in the afternoon. Grandmother was
rolling up her knitting.

"I must go home to Grandfather," she
said. "He'll be wanting his supper."

The Twins walked down the road as
far as the first bridge with Grandmother.
There she kissed them good-bye and sent
them home.

When their mother put them to bed that
night, Kat said,

"Has this been a short day, Mother?"

"Oh, very short!" said Vrouw Vedder, "because you helped me so much."

Then she kissed them good-night and went out to feed the pigs, and shut up the chickens for the night.

When she was gone, Kit said,

"I don't see how they got along before we came. We help so much!"

"No," said Kat; "I don't think —" But what she didn't think, no one will ever know, because just then she popped off to sleep.

IV
ONE SUNDAY

IV

ONE SUNDAY

ONE Sunday morning in early fall, Kit and Kat woke up and peeped out from their cupboard bed to see what was going on in the world.

The sun was shining through the little panes of the kitchen window, making square patches of light on the floor. The kettle was singing on the fire, and Vrouw Vedder was already putting away the breakfast things.

Father Vedder was lighting his pipe with a coal from the fire. He had on his black Sunday clothes, all ready for church. Father Vedder did not look at Kit and Kat at all. He just puffed away at his pipe and said to himself,

"If there are any Twins anywhere that want to go to church with me, they 'd better get dressed and eat their breakfasts."

Kit and Kat tumbled out of the cupboard at once.

Vrouw Vedder came to help them dress.

I can't tell you how many petticoats she put on Kat, but it was ever so many. And over them all she put a skirt of plaid. There was a waist of a different color, and over that a kerchief with bright red roses on it. And over the skirt she put a new, clean apron.

Kit was dressed very splendidly too. He had full baggy trousers of velveteen that reached to his ankles, and a jacket that buttoned with big silver buttons. His trousers had pockets in them.

Kit and Kat both wore stockings, which Vrouw Vedder had knit, and their best shoes of stout leather.

When they were all dressed, Vrouw Vedder stood them up side by side and had them turn around slowly to be sure they were all right.

"Now see that you behave well in meeting," she said. "Sit up straight. Look at the Dominie, and do not whisper."

"Yes, Mother," said Kit and Kat.

Then she tied a big apron over each of them and gave them each a bowl of bread and milk. While they were eating it, Father Vedder went out and looked at the pigs, and chickens, and ducks, and geese, and smoked his pipe.

When he came in, Kit and Kat were quite ready. Vrouw Vedder had tied on Kat's little white-winged cap, and put Kit's hat on. She kissed them good-bye, and they were off — one on each side of Father Vedder, holding tight to his hands.

Mother Vedder looked after them proudly, from the doorway. She did not go to church that day.

They walked slowly along the roadway in the bright sunshine. Many of their neighbors and friends, all dressed in their best, were walking to church, too.

Father Vedder and Kit and Kat went a little out of their way, in order to pass a large windmill that was swinging its arms around and creaking out a kind of sleepy windmill song. This is the song it seemed to sing : —

Around, and around, and around, I go,
Sometimes fast and sometimes slow.
I pump the water and grind the grain,
The marshy fields of the Lowlands, drain.
I harness the wind to turn my mill,
Around, and around, and around with a will!

Perhaps it was listening to the windmill song that made Kat say,

"Why do we have windmills, father?"

Kit and Kat said "Why?" every few steps on that walk. You see, they didn't often have their father all to themselves, to ask questions of.

"Why, what a little Dutch girl," said Father Vedder, "not to know what windmills are for! They pump the water out of the fields, to be sure! Don't you know how wet the fields are sometimes? If we did n't keep pumping the water out, they would be so wet we could not make gardens at all."

" Does the wind pump the water?" asked Kat.

"Of course it does, goosie girl! and grinds the grain too. The wind blows against the great arms and turns them round and round. That works the pumps; and the pumps suck the water out of the fields, and it is poured out into the canals. If it were n't for the good old windmills working away, who knows but the water would get the best of us some day and cover up all our land!"

" Would n't the dykes keep out the sea?" asked Kit.

" Suppose the dykes should break!" said Father Vedder. " Even one little break can let in lots of water. The dykes have to be watched day and night all the time, and the least bit of a hole stopped up right away, so it can't grow any bigger and let in the sea."

"Oh dear," Kat said, "what a leaky country!"

She ran near the mill and let the wind from the fans blow her hair and the white wings on her cap.

As the great fans swung near the ground, Kit jumped up and caught hold of one. It lifted him right off the ground as it swung around, and in a minute he was dangling high in the air.

"Jump, jump, quick," shouted Father Vedder.

Kit let go and dropped to the ground just in time. In another minute he would have been carried clear over.

As it was, he sat down very hard on the ground, and had to have the dirt brushed off of his Sunday clothes.

"I am surprised at you," Father Vedder said, while he brushed him. "You are too

small to swing on windmills, and besides it is the Sabbath day. Don't you ever do it again until you are big enough to be called Christopher!"

Sitting down so hard in the dirt had hurt Kit a little bit, and scared him a good deal, so he said, "No, father."

Then they walked all around the mill. They peeped inside a door which was open, and saw the pumps working away.

"Yes," said Father Vedder, "it is nip and tuck between wind and water in Holland. Let us sit down here on the canal bank, in the sunshine, and I will tell you what hard work has to be done to keep this good land of ours. And it is a good land! We should be thankful for it! Just see the rich green meadows over there, with the cows grazing in them!" — Father Vedder pointed to the beautiful fields across the canal. "The grass is so rich and fresh, that the cows here give more milk than any other cows in the whole world!"

"That's what Mother says," said Kat.

' "The Holland butter and cheese are famous everywhere," went on Father Vedder; "and we have all the good milk we want to drink, besides. The Dutch gardens, too, are the finest in the world."

"And ours is one of the best of Dutch gardens, is n't it, Father?" said Kit.

95

"It's a very good garden," said Father Vedder, proudly. "No one can raise better onions and cabbage and carrots than I can. And the Dutch bulbs! Our tulips and hyacinths make the whole world bloom!"

"Holland is really the greatest country there is; isn't it?" said Kit.

"We—ll, not in point of size, perhaps," Father Vedder admitted; "but in pluck, my boy, it is! Did you know that sometimes people call Holland the Land of Pluck?"

"I don't see why," said Kat. "I'm Dutch, but I'm afraid of lots of things! I'm afraid of spiders and of cross geese, and of falling into the water!"

"You're a girl, if you are Dutch," said Kit. "Boys are always pluckier than girls; aren't they, Father?"

"Really plucky people never boast," said Father Vedder.

Kit looked the other way and dug the toe of his shoe into the dirt. Kat snuggled up to her Father and sniffed at Kit.

"So there, Kit!" was all she said.

"There's pluck enough to go round," said Father Vedder mildly, "and we all need it —boys and girls, and men and women too. It was pluck that made Holland, and it's pluck that keeps her from slipping back into the sea."

"How did pluck make Holland?" asked Kit.

"There was n't any Holland in the first place," Father Vedder answered. " There were only some marshes and some lands under water. But people built a wall of earth around these flats; and then they pumped out the water from the space inside the wall, and made canals through the land, and drained it. And after all that work, we have our rich fields."

"How does pluck keep them?" asked Kat.

"The dykes have to be watched and mended all the time," said Father Vedder. "And the windmills have to work and work, to keep the fields drained. No one can be lazy in Holland. Each one has to work well for what he gets. If Holland should grow lazy, she would soon be back again in the Zuyder Zee! So, my children, you see you must learn well and work hard. And that is all my sermon to-day."

"It is a better sermon than the Dominie will preach, I know," said Kat.

"Tut, tut! You must never say such things," said Father Vedder. He got up and held out his hands to the Twins.

"Come! we must walk along, or we shall be late for church," he said. "Here comes the Dominie now."

There indeed was the Dominie! Kit and Kat knew him well. No one else dressed as he did. He wore a high silk hat, and long, black coat and trousers, such as city people wear.

As he came along the road, all the people bowed respectfully; the little boys took off their caps, and the little girls bobbed a courtesy. Kit and Kat bobbed and courtesied too, and the Dominie smiled at them and laid his hand on Kit's head.

"I wish he'd come to see us again," said Kit, after the Dominie had passed by.

Father Vedder was pleased.

"I am glad to see that you love your pastor, my son," he said.

"Well," said Kit, "I don't really like him so *very* much, because we have to be washed, and recite the catechism, and mind all our manners when he comes. But Mother always has such good things to eat when the Dominie comes—does n't she, Kat?—cake and preserves—and everything!"

"If it were n't for the catechism and such

things, it would be something like St. Nicholas day!" sighed Kat. "But the Dominie never forgets! And last time I could n't tell what saving grace was! The cakes are good, but —"

"Good Dutch boys and girls always learn their catechism well," said Father Vedder; "then they are glad to see the good Dominie as well as the cakes. Now no more chatter! Here is a penny for each of you to put in the bag when it is passed."

He gave them each a penny. Kit put his in his pocket. Kat did n't have a pocket, so she held hers tight in her hand.

At the church door they met Grandfather and Grandmother.

Grandfather looked very fine indeed, in his black clothes; and Grandmother was all dressed up in her best black dress, with a fresh white cap, and a shawl over her shoulders. She carried a large psalm book with golden clasps in one hand, and a scent bottle in the other. She had some peppermints too. Kit and Kat smelled them.

They all went into the church together, and an old woman led them to their seats. Kit and Kat sat one each side of Grandmother. Grandfather and Father Vedder sat on the other side of the church with all the rest of the men.

"You must sit very still and look straight before you," said Grandmother.

Kit remembered the peppermints and sat up like a soldier. So did Kat.

Pretty soon the schoolmaster came in and went up into the pulpit. He read a chapter from the Bible, and then the Dominie stood up in the pulpit and began to preach. He preached a long time.

Kit and Kat tried very hard to sit still, just as Grandmother had said; but pretty soon their heads began to nod.

Grandmother gave them each a peppermint.

They waked up for a minute. But the Dominie kept right on preaching, until they were both sound asleep with their heads on Grandmother's shoulders,—one on each side; and if they had been awake to see, they might have thought that Grandmother took a nap too.

The sermon was so very long that a great many people went to sleep. So, by and by, the Dominie said,

"We will all sing the Ninety-first Psalm."
Everybody woke up.

Grandmother opened the great golden
clasps of her psalm book, and stood up
with all the rest of the people. She stood
up quickly, so that no one would think she
had been asleep. She forgot that the Twins
were asleep too, with their heads on her
shoulders. That was why, when she got
up, Kit and Kat fell against each other and
bumped their heads !

They forgot that they were in church. They said "Ow!" both together, and Kat began to cry. But Grandmother said "Sh! sh!" and gave them each a peppermint; and that made them feel much better.

Pretty soon the schoolmaster came along with a little bag on the end of a long stick. He passed it to each person. Kit and Kat each put in a penny, though Kit had a hard time to get his out of his pocket. But Grandmother was so upset about the Twins getting bumped, that she forgot and put in a peppermint instead.

When church was over and they were out on the street again, Grandmother said,

"Now you are coming home with me to stay all night."

"Really and truly?" said the Twins. "And may we go with Grandfather to carry the milk in the morning?"

"Yes," said Grandfather, "and Kit may drive the dogs."

Kit jumped right up and down, he was so happy — even if it was Sunday.

"May I too? — May I too?" asked Kat.

"You are a girl," said Grandfather. "You may ride in the wagon."

"Oh, I wish to-morrow would come right away," said Kat.

Then Kit and Kat said good-bye to Father Vedder and went home with Grandmother and Grandfather.

They lived on a little street in the town, where the houses stood in a row close to-gether. The houses were built of brick and had wooden shutters at the windows, and they were so clean they shone in the sun.

This is a picture of Grandmother's house
and of Grandmother and Kit and Kat going
in. The door opened right into the kitchen.

Grandmother put away her shawl and
psalm book and scent bottle as soon as
she was home. Then she put on a big
apron and drew out the round table.

She boiled the kettle and made coffee;

and, when it was done, she set the coffee-pot on a pretty little porcelain stove on the table to keep hot. She got out bread and cheese and smoked beef and, best of all, a plate of little cakes.

Then they all four sat down to eat. I will not tell you how many cakes Kit and Kat ate, but it was a good many.

After dinner, Grandmother put away the things, and Kat helped her.

Kit sat beside Grandfather in the door-way while he smoked. Pretty soon Grand-father said,

"Bring me my accordeon, Kit."

Kit ran to the press in the corner. He knew where the accordeon was kept.

Then Grandfather took the accordeon, tipped his head back, shut his eyes and began to play, beating time with one foot. Kat heard the music and came out too.

She and Kit sat down on the doorstep, one on each side of Grandfather, to listen.

Grandfather played six tunes.

Then Grandmother said,

"Why don't we go to the woods to hear the band play?"

"No reason at all," said Grandfather. So very soon they were on their way to a grove on the edge of the town.

In the grove a band was playing; and just as the Twins and Grandfather and Grandmother came up, it began to play the national hymn of Holland. All the people

began to sing. There were a great many
people in the grove, and they all sang as
loud as they could; so there was a great
sound. Grandfather and Grandmother and
Kit and Kat all sang too; for they all knew
every word of the hymn.

This is what they sang: —

Let him in whom old Dutch blood flows,
Untainted, free and strong;
Whose heart for Prince and Country glows,
Now join us in our song;
Let him with us lift up his voice,
And sing in patriot band,
The song at which all hearts rejoice,
For Prince and Fatherland,
    For Prince and Fatherland.

We brothers, true unto a man,
Will sing the old song yet;
Away with him who ever can
His Prince or Land forget!
A human heart glowed in him ne'er,
We turn from him our hand,
Who callous hears the song and prayer,
For Prince and Fatherland,
    For Prince and Fatherland.

Preserve, O God, the dear old ground
Thou to our fathers gave;
The land where we a cradle found,
And where we'll find a grave!
We call, O Lord, to Thee on high,
As near death's door we stand,
Oh! Safety, blessing to our cry
For Prince and Fatherland,
 For Prince and Fatherland.

Loud ring thro' all rejoicings here,
Our prayer, O Lord, to Thee;
Preserve our Prince, his house so dear
To Holland great and free!
From youth thro' life, be this our song,
Till near to death we stand:
O God, preserve our sov'reign long,
Our Prince and Fatherland,
 Our Prince and Fatherland.

Now, while the people were singing with all their might, and the band was playing, and Kit and Kat were having the most beautiful time they had ever had in their whole lives, what do you think happened?

Down the long drive through the trees came a great, splendid carriage, drawn by

a pair of beautiful white horses with wavy white tails and manes. There were two soldiers on horseback riding in front of the carriage, and the driver of the carriage was dressed in blue and orange livery.

The carriage was open, and in it sat a beautiful, smiling young lady. Beside her sat her husband; and a nurse, in the other seat, held a baby in her arms.

When the people saw the carriage and
the lady, they waved their caps and shouted,
" Long live the Queen !,"

" Look! Look! Kit and Kat," said Grandfather. " It is your dear Queen Wilhelmina,
and Prince Henry and the little Princess !
Wave your hands !"

Kit and Kat waved with all their might,
but they were so short, and the people

crowded beside the driveway so, that neither of them could see. Then Grandfather
caught Kit and lifted him up high, and
Grandmother did the same with Kat.

It was fine to be up so high. Kit and
Kat could see everything better than any-
one else there. And when the carriage came
by, the Queen saw Kit and Kat! She smiled
at them, and the nurse held the little Princess up high for them to see! Kit and Kat
threw kisses to the little Princess; and the
Princess waved her baby hand to Kit and
Kat; and then they were all gone — like a
bright dream.

But the soldiers were better to see even
than queens, Kit thought. Kat thought the
baby — any baby — was nicer than either.

When the carriage was out of sight,
Grandfather and Grandmother set the Twins
down on the ground. Everyone began to
talk about the Queen, about how sweet she
was, and how good; and the band played,
and everybody was as happy as they could
possibly be.

By and by it was time to go home; for, Grandfather said, "Dutch girls and boys must learn to get up early in the morning, especially Twins that are going out with the milk cart."

So they went back to Grandfather Winkle's house; and Grandmother put them to bed in a little cupboard like their own at home, after they had had some supper. And the last thing Kat said that night was,

"O Kit, just to think that to-day we saw the Queen and the soldiers, and the Queen's baby, and to-morrow we are going to drive in the milk cart! What a beautiful world it is!"

Just as they were dropping off to sleep, they heard a great noise in the street.

"Clap, clap, clap," it sounded, eight times.

"There goes the Klapper-man," said Grandmother Winkle. "Eight o'clock, and time all honest folk were abed."

V

THE DAY THEY DROVE THE
MILK CART

V

THE DAY THEY DROVE THE MILK CART

THE next morning Kit and Kat woke up very early, without any one's calling them. You see, they were afraid they would be too late to go with the milk cart.

But Grandfather Winkle had only just gone out to get the milk ready, and they had plenty of time to dress while Grandmother got breakfast. Grandmother helped with the buttons and the hard parts.

Grandmother Winkle's kitchen was quite like the kitchen at home, only a little nicer. It had red tiles on the floor; and it had ever so many blue plates hanging around on the walls, and standing on edge in a row on the shelves. There was a warming-pan with a bright brass cover, hanging on the wall; and I wish you could have seen the pillows and the coverlet on the best bed!

Grandmother Winkle had embroidered those all herself, and she was very proud of them. When she had company, she always drew the curtains back so that her beautiful bed would be seen. She said that Kit and Kat were company, and she always left the curtains open when they came to visit her.

When the Twins were all dressed, Grandmother said,

"Mercy sakes! You have on your best clothes! Now that's just like a man to promise to take you out in your best clothes in a milk wagon! Whatever was Grandfather thinking about!"

Kit and Kat thought she was going to say that they couldn't go, so they dug their knuckles in their eyes and began to cry. But they hadn't got farther than the first whimper when Grandmother said,

"Well, well, we must fix it somehow. Don't cry now, that's a good Kit and Kat." So the Twins took their knuckles out of their eyes and began to smile.

Grandmother went to the press and brought out two aprons. One was a very small apron. It would n't reach to Kit's knees. But she put it on him and tied it around his waist.

"This was your Uncle Jan's when he was a little boy," she said. "It's pretty small, but it will help some."

Kit wished that Uncle Jan had taken it with him when he went to America. But he did n't say so.

Then Grandmother took another apron out of the press. It looked as if it had been there a long time.

"Kat, you must wear this," she said. "It was your mother's when she was a little girl."

Now, this apron was all faded, and it had patches on it of different kinds of cloth. Kat looked at her best dress. Then she looked at the apron. Then she thought about the milk cart. She wondered if she

wanted to go in the milk cart badly enough
to wear that apron over her Sunday dress!
She stuck her finger in her mouth and
looked sidewise at Grandmother Winkle.

Grandmother didn't say a word. She
just looked firm and held up the apron.

Very soon Kat came slowly — very
slowly — and Grandmother buttoned the
apron up behind, and that was the end of
that.

The Twins could hardly eat any breakfast, they were in such a hurry to go. As
soon as they had taken the last spoonful,
and Grandfather Winkle had finished his
coffee, they ran out into the place where
the dogs were kept, to help Grandfather
harness them.

There were two black and white dogs.
Their names were Peter and Paul.

The wagon was small, just the right size
for the dogs; and it was painted blue. The
bright brass cans full of milk were already
in; and there was a little seat for Kat to
sit on.

When the last strap was fastened, Grandfather lifted Kat up and set her on the seat.
She held on with both hands.

Then Grandfather gave the lines to Kit,
and a little stick for a whip, and told him
to walk slowly along beside the dogs. He
told him to be sure not to let go of the
lines.

Grandfather walked behind, carrying some milk cans.

Grandmother stood in the door to see them off; and, as they started away, Kat took one hand off the cart long enough to wave it to her. Then she held on again; for the bricks in the pavement made the cart joggle a good deal.

"We must go first to Vrouw de Vet," Grandfather called out. "She takes one quart of milk. Go slowly."

At first Kit went slowly. But pretty soon there was a great rattling behind him; and Hans Hite, a boy he knew, drove right past him with his dog cart! He drove fast; and, as he passed Kit, he stuck out his tongue and called out,

"Milk for sale! Milk for sale!
A milk cart drawn by a pair of snails!"

Kit forgot all about going slowly.

"Get up!" he said to the dogs, and he touched them with his long stick.

Peter and Paul "got up." They jumped forward and began to run!

Kit ran as fast as his legs would go beside the dogs, holding the lines. But the dogs had four legs apiece, and Kit had only two; so you see he could n't keep up very well.

Kat began to scream the moment that Peter and Paul began to run. The dogs thought that something that made a dreadful noise was after them, and they ran faster than ever. You see, Grandfather Winkle never in the world screamed like that, and Peter and Paul did n't know what to make of it. So they ran and ran and ran.

Kat held on the best she could, but she bounced up ever so far in the air every time the cart struck a bump in the street. So did the milk cans ; and when they came down again, the milk splashed out.

Kat did n't always come down in the same spot. All the spots were hard, so it did n't really matter much which one she struck as she came down.

But Kat did n't think about that; she just screamed. And Peter and Paul ran and ran, and Kit ran and ran, until he could n't run any more; he just sat down hard on the pavement and slid along. But he did n't let go of the lines !

When Kit sat down, it jerked the dogs so hard that they stopped suddenly. But Kat did n't stop; she went right on. She flew out over the front of the cart and landed on the ground, among all of Peter and Paul's legs! Then she stopped going, but she didn't stop screaming.

And, though Kit was a boy, he screamed some too. Then Peter and Paul pointed their noses up in the air and began to howl.

Way back, ever so far, Grandfather was coming along as fast as he could; but that wasn't very fast.

All the doors on the street flew open, and all the good housewives came clattering out to see what was the matter. They picked Kat up and told her not to cry, and wiped her eyes with their aprons, and stood Kit on his feet, and patted the dogs; and pretty soon Peter and Paul stopped barking, and Kit and Kat stopped screaming, and then it was time to find out what had really happened.

Neither of the Twins had any broken bones; the good housewives wiggled all their arms and legs, and felt of their bones to see. But shocking things had happened, nevertheless! Kat had torn a great hole in the front of her best dress; and Kit had

worn two round holes in the seat of his
Sunday clothes, where he slid along on the
pavement; and, besides that, the milk was
slopped all over the bottom of the cart!

Just then Grandfather came up. If it
had n't been that his pipe was still in his
mouth, I really don't know what he might
not have said! He looked at the cart, and
he looked at the Twins. Then he took his
pipe out of his mouth and said sternly to
Kit,

"Why didn't you do as I told you?"

"I did," said Kit, very much scared.
"You told me to be sure to hold tight to
the lines, and I did! I never let go once."

"Yes, and look at his clothes," said one
of the women. She turned him around and
showed Grandfather the holes.

"I told you to go slowly," said Grandfather. "Now look at the cart, and see what
you've done by not minding, — spoiled
your best clothes and Kat's, and spilled the
milk ! Go back to Grandmother."

"But I could n't mind twice at one time,"
said Kit. "I was minding about not letting
go."

"Oh dear," sobbed Kat, "I wish we were
four and a half feet high now ! If we were,
this never would have happened."

Grandfather took the dogs and went on
to Vrouw de Vets, without another word.

The Twins took each other's hands, and
walked back to Grandmother's house. Quite
a number of little boys and girls in wooden
shoes clattered along with them. Grand-

mother heard all the noise, and ran to the door to see what was the matter.

"Laws a mercy me, I told you so!" she cried, the moment she saw them. "Look at your clothes! See how you 've torn them!"

"I *can't* see the holes in mine," said Kit.

"But I can," said Kat. And then all the children talked at once; and what with wooden shoes and the tongues all going, Grandmother clapped her hands over her ears to shut out the noise. Then she took Kit and Kat into the kitchen and shut the door. She put on her glasses and got down on the floor so she could see better.

Then she turned Kit and Kat all around and looked at the holes. "O! my soul!" she said. She took off the aprons and the torn clothes and put the Twins to bed while she mended.

She got out a pair of Grandfather's oldest velveteen breeches that had been patched a great deal, and found a good piece to patch with. Then she patched the holes in

Kit's breeches so neatly that one had to look very carefully indeed to see that there had ever been any holes there at all.

Then she patched Kat's dress; and, when it was all done, she shook it out and said to herself,

"Seems to me those Twins have been quiet for a long time."

She went over to the cupboard bed; and there were Kit and Kat fast asleep, with their cheeks all stained with tears and dirt. Grandmother Winkle kissed them. Kit and Kat woke up, and Grandmother dressed them in their Sunday clothes again, and washed their faces and made them feel as good as new.

By and by Grandfather Winkle came home from going about with the milk. Grandmother Winkle scrubbed the cart and made it all clean again; and by noon you would never have known, unless you had looked very, very closely — much more closely than would be polite — that anything had happened to the Twins or the milk cart, or their clothes or anything.

After they had eaten their dinner, and the dogs were rested and Grandfather had smoked his pipe he said,

"Kit, if you think you can mind, I will take you and Kat both home in the dog cart." Kit and Kat both nodded their heads ·very hard. "Only, I'll do the driving myself," said Grandfather Winkle. And he did.

He put Kit and Kat both on the seat, and

he walked slowly beside the cart. They
went out on the road beside the canal toward home. They got there just as the sun
was getting low in the west, and Vrouw
Vedder was going out to feed her chickens.

VI

THE DAY THEY GOT THEIR SKATES

VI

THE DAY THEY GOT THEIR SKATES

ONE morning, when Kit and Kat ran out early to feed their ducklings, the frost nipped their noses and ears.

"It's getting colder every day. Very soon winter will come," Kat said.

They ran down to the canal. The old goose and the gander and the goslings — now half grown — were standing on the bank, looking unhappy: there was a thin sheet of ice all over the canal, and they could not go swimming.

Kit took a stick and broke the ice. Thin sheets of it, like pieces of broken glass, were soon floating about; and the old goose, the gander, and all the goslings went down the bank in a procession into the water.

139

They swam about among the pieces of ice for a while, but it was so cold that they soon came up on the bank into the sun again and wiggled their tails to shake out the water. Then they all sat down in the sun to get their feet warm.

Kit and Kat ran up and down the road and played tag until their cheeks were red and they were warm as toast. Then they ran into Vrouw Vedder's warm kitchen.

The kettle was singing on the fire, and there was a smell of coffee in the air. Vrouw Vedder gave the Twins some in a large cup. She put in a good deal of milk and gave them each a piece of sugar to sweeten it with.

" Is it Sunday ?" asked Kat. On Sundays they sometimes had coffee. On other days they had milk.

" No," said Vrouw Vedder; "but it is cold, and I thought a cup of coffee would warm us all up."

While they were drinking their coffee,

Kit and Kat talked about the ice, and what fun they would have with their sleds on the canals when winter came.

"I tell you what it is, Kat," said Kit; "I think we're big enough to have skates. Hans Hite isn't much bigger than I am, and he had skates last winter. I mean to ask Father this very day."

"Yah," said Kat — that is the way Dutch Twins always say yes — "Yah, and let us be very good and help mother all we can. I think maybe they will give skates to good Twins quite soon, even if we aren't very big yet — not big enough to be called Christopher and Katrina."

Vrouw Vedder was heating water and getting out her scrubbing brushes, so Kit and Kat knew that she was going to clean something.

"What are you going to scrub to-day, Mother?" asked Kit.

"I'm going to scrub the stable," said Vrouw Vedder. "It is getting too cold for the cows to stay all night in the pastures.

Father means to bring Mevrouw Holstein in to-night, and I want her stable to be nice and clean for her."

"We'll help you," said Kit and Kat very politely.

"Good children!" their mother said. "You may carry the brushes." So they opened a door beside the fireplace, and walked right into the stable.

The stable was really a part of the house. There were two stalls in the stable. Vrouw Vedder took her pails of water and her brushes and began to scrub. She scrubbed the walls, and the sides of the stalls, and the floor. The Twins scrubbed, too, until they were tired; and the stable was so clean, you would have liked to live there yourself.

"Let's play out here," said Kat. "Let's play house."

"All right," said Kit. "I'll be the father, and you be the mother."

"But who will be Twins?" said Kat.

"Let's get the ducklings," said Kit.

"They can be Twins, of course," said Kat. "They are, anyway."

So Kit ran out and brought in the ducklings. They were so tame they always ran to Kit and Kat, when they saw them coming. They were almost ducks now, they had grown so big.

"Let's give the Twins their dinner," said Kat. So she got some grain, and they both sat down on a little box and held the ducks in their laps and fed them from their hands. The ducks ate greedily.

"You have very bad manners," said Kat. "You will get your clothes all dirty." She took two rags and tied them around the ducks' necks for bibs. The ducks did not like bibs. They quacked.

"Now don't say anything like that," said Kat. "You must do just as you are told and not spill your food."

Then Kit got some water and a spoon and gave the Twins a drink, but they did not like the drink either.

"Now we must put them to sleep," said

143

Kat. They rocked the ducks in their arms, but the ducks squawked dreadfully.

"What bad children to cry so!" said Kit. "You can have both the Twins"; and he gave his duck to Kat.

"You fix a bed for them," said Kat. So Kit turned up the box they had been sitting on, and put some hay in it; and they put the ducks in on the hay.

Pretty soon the ducks went to sleep. Kit and Kat ran away to play out of doors and forgot all about them.

They did n't think about them again until Father Vedder came home at night with Mevrouw Holstein. When he put the cow into the stall, he stumbled over the box. It was rather dark in the stable.

"Quack, quack!" said the ducks.

Kit and Kat were helping Father put the cow into the stall and get some hay for her. When the ducks quacked, Father Vedder said,

"What in the world is this?"

"Oh, our Twins! our Twins!" cried Kit and Kat. "Don't let Mevrouw Holstein step on the Twins!"

Father Vedder pulled out the box. Kit and Kat each took a duck and carried it out to the poultry house.

"Twins are a great care," said Kit and Kat.

"Now is the time to ask," whispered Kat to Kit, that night, when Father Vedder had finished his supper and was lighting his pipe. "You must ask very politely,—just the very politest way you can."

They went and stood before their father. They put their feet together. Kit made a bow, and Kat bobbed a curtsy.

"Dear parent," said Kit.

"That's a good start," whispered Kat. "Go on."

"Well, well, what now?" said Father Vedder.

"Dear parent, Kat and I are quite big now. I think we must be *nearly* four feet and a half high. Don't you think we are big enough to have skates this winter?"

"So that's it!" said Father Vedder. Then he smoked his pipe again.

"There was ice on the canal this morning," said Kat.

"So you think you are big enough to skate, do you?" said Father Vedder, at last. Mother Vedder was clearing away the supper. "What do you think about it, Mother?" said Father Vedder.

"They have been very good children," said the Vrouw. "There are the skates you and I had when we were children. We might

146

try them on and see if they are big enough
to wear them. They are in the bag hanging
back of the press."

Kit and Kat almost screamed with joy.

"Our feet are quite large. I'm sure we
can wear them," they said.

Father Vedder got the bag down and took
out two pairs of skates. They had long curl-
ing ends on the runners. The Twins sat down
on the floor. Father Vedder tried on the
skates.

"They are still pretty large; but you will
grow," he told the Twins. "You may have

147

them if you will be very careful and not let them get rusty. By and by we will teach you to skate."

The Twins practiced standing in the skates on the kitchen floor; and, when bedtime came, they took the skates to bed with them.

"O Kit," said Kat, "I never supposed we'd get them so soon. Did you?"

"Well," said Kit, "you see, we're pretty big and *very* good. That makes a difference."

"It's very nice to be good when people notice it, isn't it?" said Kat.

"Yah," said Kit. "I'm going to be good now right along, all the time; for very soon St. Nicholas will come, and he leaves only a rod in the shoes of bad children. And if you've been bad, you have to tell him about it."

"Oh! Oh!" said Kat. "I'm going to be good all the time too. I'm going to be good until after the feast of St. Nicholas, anyway."

Not many days after Kit and Kat got their skates, there came a cold, cold wind. It blew over the fields and over the canals all day and all night long; and in the morning, when the Twins looked out, the canal was one shining roadway of ice.

Father Vedder came in from the stable with a great pail full of milk.

"Winter is here now, for good and all," he said, as he set the pail down. "The canals are frozen over, and soon it will be the day for the feast of St. Nicholas."

Kit and Kat ran to him and said, both together,

"Dear Father Vedder, will you *please* teach us to skate before St. Nicholas Day?"

"I'll see if the ice is strong enough to bear," said Father Vedder; and he went right down to the canal to see, that very minute. When he came in, he said,

"Yes, the ice is strong; and we will go out as soon as you are ready, and try your skates."

Vrouw Vedder said,

"I should like to go too"; and Father Vedder said to Kit and Kat,

"Your mother used to be the finest skater in the whole village when she was a young girl. You must not let her beat you."

They hurried through with their work — Kit and Kat helped. Then they all put on their heavy shoes and wraps, took their skates over their shoulders, and started for the canal.

"If you learn to skate well enough, we will take you to town before the feast of St. Nicholas," said Father Vedder. "But it comes very soon."

He put on his own skates and Kit's, and the mother put on her own and Kat's.

"I'm sure we can do it almost right away," said Kat.

"Now we'll show you how to skate," said Father Vedder. He stood the Twins up on the ice. They held each other's hands. They were afraid to move. Father Vedder took Mother Vedder's hand.

"See," he said, "like this!" And away

they went like two swallows, skimming over
the ice. In a minute they were ever so far
away.

Kit and Kat felt lonesome, and very
queer, when they saw their father and
mother flying along in that way. They
were n't used to see them do anything but
work, and move about slowly.

" It looks easy," said Kit. "Let 's try it.
We must not be afraid."

He started with his right leg, pushing it
out a little in front of him. But it was very
strange how his legs acted. They did n't

seem to belong to him at all! His left leg tried to follow his right, just as it ought to; but, instead, it slid out sidewise and knocked against Kat's skates. Then both Kat's feet flew up; and she sat down very hard, on the ice. And Kit came down on top of her.

They tried to get up; but, each time they tried, their feet slid away from them.

"Oh dear," said Kat, "we are all mixed up! Are those your feet or mine? I can't tell which is which!"

"They don't any of them mind," said Kit. "I can't stand up on any of them. I've tried them all! We'll just have to wait until Father and Mother come back and pick us out."

"Ice is quite cold to sit on, isn't it?" said Kat.

Soon Father and Mother Vedder came skimming back again. When they saw Kit and Kat, they laughed and skated to them, picked them up, and set them on their feet.

"Now I'll take Kit, and you take Kat,"

said Vrouw Vedder to her husband, "and they'll be skating in no time." So Kat's father took her hands, and Kit took hold of his mother's, and they started off.

At first the Twins' feet did n't behave well at all. They seemed to want to do everything they could to bother them. They would sprawl way apart; then they would toe in and run into each other.

Many times Kit and Kat would have fallen if Father and Mother Vedder had not held them up; but before the lesson was over, both Kit and Kat could skate a little bit alone.

"See, this is the way," said Vrouw Vedder; and she skated around in a circle. Then she cut a figure like this ∞ in the ice. Then Father Vedder did a figure like this ∽ all on one foot.

"My!" said Kit and Kat.

"I think our parents must skate the best of all the people in the world," said Kat.

"I'm going to some day," said Kit.

"So'm I," said Kat.

After a while Vrouw Vedder said,

"It's time to go home. Not too much the first time." So they all went back home with their cheeks as red as roses, and their noses too, and *such* an appetite for dinner!

But the Twins were a little lame next day.

Every day after that, Kit and Kat went out with their skates to the ditches and tried and tried to skate as Father and Mother did —they did so want to skate to town and see the sights before the feast of St. Nicholas! They worked so hard that in a week they could skate very well; and then they planned a surprise for their mother.

"If you will watch at the window, you'll see a great sight on the canal very soon," said Kit to his mother one day.

Of course Vrouw Vedder had n't the least idea what it would be!

Kit and Kat slipped out through the stable and ran down to the ditch. They put on their skates and skated from the ditch out to the big canal.

Vrouw Vedder was watching at the window. Soon she saw Kit and Kat go flying by, hand in hand, on the canal! They waved their hands to her. Vrouw Vedder was so pleased that she went to call Father Vedder, who was in the hay-loft over the stable.

"Come and see Kit and Kat," she cried.

Father Vedder came down from the loft and looked too. Then Kit cut a figure like this, ⟰, and Kat cut one like this, ●⟩. The round spot is where she sat down hard, just as she was almost around.

When they came into the kitchen Father said,

"I think we could take such a fine pair of skaters as that to the Vink with us on our way to town! The ice is very hard and thick for so early in the season, and we will go to-morrow."

"We can see the shops too. St. Nicholas is coming, and the shops are full of fine things," said Vrouw Vedder.

Kit and Kat could hardly wait for to-morrow to come. They polished their skates and made everything ready.

"What do you suppose the Vink is?" said Kat to Kit.

"I think it is something like a church," said Kit.

"You don't know what a Vink is — so there," said Kat. "*I* think it's something to eat."

Then Kit changed the subject.

"I'll race you to-morrow," he said.

"I'll beat," said Kat.

"We'll see," said Kit.

The next day they started, all four, quite early in the morning. Vrouw Vedder took her basket on her arm.

"I shall want to buy some things," she said.

Father Vedder lighted his pipe—"To keep my nose warm," he said.

Then they all went down to the canal and put on their skates.

"Kat and I are going to race to the first windmill," said Kit.

"I'll tell you when to start," said Father
Vedder.

"And I'll get a cake for the one who
wins," said the mother.

"One, two, three!" Away they flew like
the wind! Father and Mother Vedder came
close behind.

Kit was so sure he would beat that he thought he would show off a little. He went zigzag across the canal; once or twice he stopped to skate in curves.

Kat did n't stop for anything. She kept her eyes on the windmill, and she skated as hard as she could.

They were getting quite near the mill now. Kit stopped playing and began to skate as fast as he could. But Kat had got the start of him.

"I 'll soon get ahead of her," he thought. "She 's a girl, and I 'm a boy." He struck out with great long sweeps — as long as such short legs could make — but Kat kept ahead; and in another minute there she was at the windmill, quite out of breath, and pointing her finger at Kit!

"I beat — I beat," she said.

"Well, I could have beaten if I wanted to," said Kit.

"I 'll get the cake," said Kat.

"I don't care," said Kit. But Kat knew that he did.

"I'll give you a piece," she said.

Father and Mother Vedder came along then; and when Kit and Kat were rested, they all skated for a long time without saying anything. Then Father Vedder said proudly to his wife,

"They keep up as well as anybody! Were there ever such Twins!" And Mother Vedder said,

"Never!"

By and by other people appeared on the canal — men and women and children, all skating. They were going to the town to see the sights too.

One woman skated by with her baby in her arms. One man was smoking a long pipe, and his wife was carrying a basket of eggs. But the man and woman were good skaters. They flew along, laughing; and no one could get near enough to upset them.

As they came nearer to the town, Kit and Kat saw a tent near the place where one canal opened into another. A man stood

near the tent. He put his hands together
and shouted through them to the skaters,

"Come in, come in, and get a drink
  Of warm sweet milk on your way to the Vink."

"We must be getting quite near the Vink," Kat said. "I do wonder what it looks like! Do you think it's alive?"

They passed another tent. There a man was shouting,

"Come buy a sweet cake; it costs but a cent,
  Come buy, come buy, from the man in the tent."

Vrouw Vedder said,

"I promised a cake to the one who beat in the race. We'll go in here and get it."

So they went to the tent.

They bought two cakes, and each ate half of one. Kat broke the cakes and gave them to the others, because she won the race.

When they had eaten the cakes, they skated on. The canals grew more and more crowded. There were a good many tents; flags were flying, and the whole place was very gay.

At last they saw a big building, with crowds of merry skaters about it. Many people were going in and out.

"There 's the Vink," said Father Vedder.

"Where?" said Kit and Kat.

He pointed to the building.

"Oh!" said Kit. He never said another word about what they had thought it was like.

Soon they were inside the "Vink." It was a large restaurant. There were many little tables about, crowded with people, eating and drinking. Father Vedder found a table, and they all sat down.

"Bring us some pea soup," he said to the waiter. Soon they were eating the hot soup.

"This is the best thing I ever had," said Kit.

When they had eaten their soup, they went out of the building and walked through the streets of the town. All the shops were filled with pretty things. The bake shops had wonderful cakes with little candies on top, and there were great cakes made like St. Nicholas himself in his long robes.

Kit and Kat flattened their noses against all the shop windows, and looked at the toys and cakes.

"I wish St. Nicholas would bring me

that," said Kit, pointing to a very large St. Nicholas cake.

"And I want some of those," Kat said, pointing to some cakes made in the shapes of birds and fish.

Vrouw Vedder had gone with her basket on an errand. Father Vedder and Kit and Kat walked slowly along, waiting for her.

Soon there was a great noise up the street.
There were shouts, and the clatter of wooden
shoes.

"Look! Look!" cried Kit.

There, in the midst of the crowd, was a
great white horse; and riding on it was the
good St. Nicholas himself! He had a long

white beard and red cheeks, and long robes, with a mitre on his head; and he smiled at the children, who crowded around him and followed him in a noisy procession down the street.

Behind St. Nicholas came a cart, filled with packages of all sizes. The children were all shouting at once, "Give me a cake, good St. Nicholas!" or, "Give me a new pair of shoes!" or whatever each one wanted most.

"Where is he going?" asked Kit and Kat.

"He's carrying presents to houses where there are good girls and boys," Father Vedder said. "For bad children, there is only a rod in the shoe."

"I'm glad we're so good," said Kit.

"When will he come to our house?" asked Kat.

"Not until to-morrow," said Father Vedder. "But you must fill your wooden shoes with beans or hay for his good horse, to-night; and then perhaps he will come down the chimney and leave something in them. It's worth trying."

Kit and Kat were in a hurry to get home, for fear the Saint would get there first.

It was growing late, so they all went to a waffle shop for their supper.

In the shop a woman sat before an open fire. On the fire was a big waffle iron. She made the waffles, put sugar and butter on them, and passed a plate of them to each one. Oh, how good they were!

When they had eaten their waffles, Father
and Mother Vedder and the Twins went
back to the canal and put on their skates.
It was late in the afternoon. They took
hold of hands and began to skate toward
home, four in a row. Father and Mother
Vedder were on the outside, and the Twins
in the middle.

It was dark when they reached home.
Vrouw Vedder lighted the fire, while Father
Vedder went to feed the cow and see that
the chickens and ducks and geese were all
safe for the night.

Kit and Kat ran for their wooden shoes.
They each took one and put some hay in

167

it. This was for St. Nicholas to give to his horse. Father Vedder put the shoes on the mantel. Then they hurried to bed to make morning come quicker.

Father and Mother Vedder sat up late that night. Mother Vedder said it was to prepare the goose for dinner the next day.

When the Twins woke the next morning, the fire was already roaring up the chimney, and the kitchen was warm as toast. They hopped out of bed and ran for their wooden shoes. Mother Vedder reached up to the mantel shelf for them. Truly, the hay was gone — and there in each shoe was a package done up in paper!

"Oh, he *did* come! He *did* come!" cried Kat. "O Mother, you're sure you did n't build the fire before he had got out of the chimney?"

"I'm sure," said Vrouw Vedder. "I've made the fire on many a St. Nicholas morning, and I've never burned him yet!"

The Twins climbed up the steps to their cupboard bed and sat on the edge of it to

open their packages. In Kit's was a big St. Nicholas cake, like the one in the shop window! And in Kat's were three cakes like birds, and two like fish!

"Just what we wanted!" said Kit and Kat. "Do you suppose he heard us say so?"

"St. Nicholas can hear what people *think*," said Vrouw Vedder. "He is coming to see you to-night at six o'clock, and you must be ready to sing him a little song and answer any questions he asks you."

"How glad I am that we are so good!" said Kat.

"We'll see what the Saint thinks about that," said the mother. "Now get dressed; for Grandfather and Grandmother will be here for dinner, and we're going to have roast goose, and there's a great deal to do."

Kit and Kat set their beautiful cakes up where they could see them while they dressed.

"I do wish every day were St. Nicholas Day," said Kit.

"Or the day before," said Kat. "That was such a nice day!"

"*All* the days are nice days, I think," said Kit.

"I don't think the dog-cart day was so very nice," said Kat. "We tore our best clothes, and they'll never, never be so nice again. That was because *you* did n't mind!"

"Well," said Kit, "I minded as much as

I could. How can I mind two things at one time? You know how well I can think! You know how I thought about Vrouw Van der Kloot's cakes. But I *can't* think how I can mind twice at one time."

"I don't suppose you can," said Kat. "But anyway, I'm sorry about my dress."

Just then Vrouw Vedder called them to come and eat their breakfast.

Father and Mother Vedder sat down at the little round table and bowed their heads. Kit and Kat stood up. Father Vedder said grace; and then they ate their salt herring and

drank their coffee; and Kit and Kat had coffee
too, because it was St. Nicholas morning.

It was snowing when, after breakfast, Kit
went out with his father to feed the chickens
and the pigs, and to see that the cow had
something very good that she liked to eat.
When they had done that, they called Kat; and
she helped throw out some grain on the white
snow, so the birds could have a feast, too.

It snowed all day. Kit and Kat both

helped their mother get the dinner. They got the cabbage and the onions and the potatoes ready; and when the goose was hung upon the fire to roast, they watched it and kept it spinning around on the spit, so it would brown evenly.

By and by the kitchen was all in order, and you can't think how clean and homelike it looked! The brasses all around the room had little flames dancing in them, because they were so bright and shiny. Everything was ready for the St. Nicholas feast. The goose was nearly roasted, and there was such a good smell of it in the air!

After a while there was a great stamping of feet at the door; and Vrouw Vedder ran with the broom to brush the snow off Grandfather and Grandmother, who had skated all the way from town, on the canal. When they were warmed and dried, and all their wraps put away, Grandfather and Grandmother Winkle looked around the pleasant kitchen; and Grandmother said to Grandfather.

"Our Neltje is certainly a good house-wife." Neltje was Vrouw Vedder. And Grandfather said,

"There's only one better one, my dear." He meant Grandmother Winkle.

By and by they all sat down to dinner, and I can't begin to tell you how good it was! It makes one hungry just to think of it. They had roast goose and onions and turnips and cabbage. They had bread and butter, and cheese, and sweet cakes.

"Everything except the flour in the bread, we raised ourselves," said Vrouw Vedder. "The hens gave us the eggs; and the cow, the butter. The Twins helped Father and me to take care of the chickens, and to milk the cow, and to make the butter; so it is our very own St. Nicholas feast that we are eating."

"A farmer's life is the best life there is," said Father Vedder.

They sat a long time at the table; and Grandfather told stories about when he was a boy; and Father Vedder told how Kit and

Kat learned to skate; and Kit and Kat told
how they saw St. Nicholas riding on a white
horse, and how he sent them the very things
they wanted; and they all enjoyed themselves very much.

After dinner, Grandmother Winkle sat
down in the chimney corner and called Kit
and Kat.

"Come here," she said, "and I'll tell you
some stories about St. Nicholas."

The Twins brought two little stools and sat beside her, one on each side. She took out her knitting; and as the needles clicked in her fingers, she told this story:

"Once upon a time, many years ago, three little brothers went out one day to the woods to gather fagots. They were just about as big as you are, Kit and Kat."

"Were they all three, twins?" asked Kat.

"The story doesn't tell about that," said Grandmother Winkle; "but maybe they were. At any rate, they all got lost in the woods and wandered ever so far, trying to find their way home. But instead of finding their way home, they just got more and more lost all the time. They were very tired and hungry; but, as they were brave boys, not one of them cried."

"It's lucky that none of those twins were girls," said Kit.

"I've even heard of boy twins that cried, when dog carts ran away, or something of that kind happened," said Grandmother

Winkle. "But you should n't interrupt; it's not polite."

"Oh!" said Kit very meekly.

"Well, as I was saying, they were very lost indeed. Night was coming on; and they were just thinking that they must lie down on the ground to sleep, when one of them saw a light shining through the leaves. He pointed it out to the others; and they walked along toward it, stumbling over roots and stones as they went, for it was now quite dark.

"As they came nearer, they saw that the light came from the window of a poor little hut on the edge of a clearing.

"They went to the door and knocked. The door was opened by a dirty old woman, who lived in the hut with her husband, who was a farmer.

"The boys told the old woman that they had lost their way, and asked her if she could give them a place to sleep. She spoke to her husband, who sat crouched over a little fire in the corner; and he told her to give them a bed in the loft.

The three boys climbed the little ladder into the loft and lay down on the hay. They were so tired that they fell asleep at once. The old man and his wife whispered about them over their bit of fire.

"'They are fine-looking boys; and well dressed,' said the old woman.

"'Yes,' said the old man, 'and I have no doubt they have plenty of money about them.'

"'Do you really think so?' said the wife.

"'I think I'll find out,' said the wicked farmer. So he climbed up to the loft and killed the three boys. Then he looked in their pockets for money; but there was no money there.

"He was very angry. And he was very much afraid—wicked people are always afraid."

"Are all afraid people wicked?" asked Kat. She wished very much that she were brave.

"M-m-m, well—not *always*," said Grandmother Winkle.

"The wicked farmer was so afraid that he wanted to put the bodies of the three boys where no one would find them. So he carried them down cellar and put them into the pickle tub with his pork."

"Oh! Oh! Oh!" screamed Kat, and she put her hands over her ears. Even Kit's eyes were very round and big. But Grandmother said,

"Now, don't you be scared until I get to the end of the story. Did n't I tell you it was all about St. Nicholas? You wait and see what happened!

"That very same day the wicked farmer went to market with some vegetables to sell. As he was sitting in the market, St. Nicholas appeared before him. He had on his mitre and his long robes, just as you see him in Kit's cake.

" 'Have you any pork to sell?' St. Nicholas asked the man.

" 'No,' said the farmer.

" 'What of the three young pigs in your brine tub in the cellar?' said St. Nicholas.

179

"The farmer saw that his wicked deed was found out—as all wicked deeds are, sooner or later. He fell on his knees and begged the good Saint to forgive him.

"St. Nicholas said, 'Show me the way to your house.'

"The farmer left his vegetables unsold in the market and went home at once, the Saint following all the way.

"When they reached the hut, St. Nicholas went to the pickled-pork tub in 'the cellar. He waved his staff over the tub, and out jumped the three boys, hearty and well! Then the good Saint took them through the woods and left them in sight of their own home."

"Oh, what a good St. Nicholas!" said Kit and Kat. "Tell us another."

"Well," said Grandmother Winkle, "once upon another time there was a very mean man, who had a great deal of money—that often happens. He had, also, three beautiful daughters — that sometimes happens too.

"One day he lost all his money. Now, he cared more for money than for anything else in the world — more, even, than for his three beautiful daughters. So he made up his mind to sell them!

"St. Nicholas knew of this wicked plan; so that very night he went to the man's house and dropped some money through a broken window."

"Why did he do that?" asked Kat.

"Because the man was selling his daughters to get money. If he had money enough, he would n't sell them.

"The first night St. Nicholas dropped enough money to pay for the eldest daughter. The next night he took a purse of gold for the second daughter, and dropped it down the chimney. It fell down right in front of the man, as he was getting a coal to light his pipe. The third night the man watched; and when St. Nicholas came, the door flew open, and the man ran out. He caught St. Nicholas by his long robe and held him.

"'O St. Nicholas, Servant of the Lord,'

he said, 'why dost thou hide thy good deeds?'

"And from that time on, every one has known it is St. Nicholas who brings gifts in the night and drops them down the chimney."

"Did the man sell his daughter?" asked Kat.

"No," said Grandmother. "He was so ashamed of himself that he wasn't wicked any more."

"Does St. Nicholas give everybody presents so they will be good?" asked Kat.

"Yes," said Grandmother; "that's why bad children get only a rod in their shoes."

"He gave the bad man nice presents to make him good," said Kit. "Why doesn't he give bad children nice things to make *them* good too?"

Grandmother Winkle knitted for a minute without speaking. Then she said,

"I guess he thinks that the rod is the present that will make them good in the shortest time."

The clock had been ticking steadily along while Grandmother had been telling stories, and it was now late in the afternoon. The sky was all red in the west; there were long, long shadows across the snowy fields, and the corners of the kitchen were quite dark.

"It's almost time to expect him, now," said Vrouw Vedder; and she brought out a sheet and spread it in the middle of the kitchen floor. She stirred up the fire, and the room was filled with the pleasant glow from the flames.

Kit and Kat sat on their little stools. Their eyes were very big. At five minutes of six, Vrouw Vedder said,

"He will be here in just a few minutes, now. Get up, Kit and Kat, and sing your song!"

The Twins stood up on the edge of the sheet and began to sing:

> "St. Nicholas, good, holy man,
> Put on your best gown;
> Ride with it to Amsterdam,
> From Amsterdam to Spain."

While they were singing, there was a
sound at the door, of some one feeling for
the latch. Then the door flew open, and a
great shower of sweet cakes and candies fell

onto the sheet, all around Kit and Kat!
There in the doorway stood St. Nicholas
himself, smiling and shaking off the snow!
His horse was stamping outside. Kit and
Kat could hear it.

They stopped singing and hardly breathed,
—they stood so still. They looked at St.
Nicholas with big, big eyes. In one hand
St. Nicholas carried two large packages; in
the other, a birch rod.

"Are there any good children here?" said
St. Nicholas.

"Pretty good, if you please, dear St.
Nicholas," said Kit in a very small
voice.

"Children who always mind their mothers
and fathers and grandfathers and grand-
mothers?" said St. Nicholas, "and who do
not quarrel?"

Kat couldn't say anything at all, though
the Saint looked right at her! Vrouw Vedder
spoke.

"I think, dear St. Nicholas, they are very
good children," she said.

"Then I will leave these for them and carry the rod along to some bad little boy and girl, if I find one," said St. Nicholas. "There seem to be very few about here. I have n't left a single rod yet." And he handed one big package to Kit, and another to Kat.

"Thank you," said Kit and Kat.

St. Nicholas smiled at them and waved his hand. Then the door shut, and he was gone!

Kit and Kat dropped on their knees to pick up the cakes and candies. They passed the cakes and candies around to each one. Vrouw Vedder lighted the candles, and then they all gathered around to see Kit and Kat open their bundles.

"You open yours first," said Vrouw Vedder to Kat.

Kat was so excited that she could hardly untie the string. When she got the bundle open, there was a beautiful new Sunday dress—much prettier than the torn one had ever been! Oh, how pleased Kat was! She

hugged her mother and her grandmother and her father and her grandfather.

"I just wish I could hug dear St. Nicholas, too," she said.

Then Kit opened his bundle; and there was a beautiful new velveteen suit, with his very own silver buttons on it! It had pockets in it! He put his hand in one pocket.

It had a penny in it! Then he put his hand in the other pocket. There was another penny!

"I'm going to see if there's a pocket in mine," said Kat.

She hunted and hunted and hunted. By and by she found a pocket. And sure enough, there was a penny in that too!

Then some presents came from somewhere for Father and Mother Vedder and for Grandfather and Grandmother Winkle; and such a time as they all had, opening the bundles and showing their presents!

Then Mother Vedder tried on Kit's suit and Kat's dress, to see if they were the right size. They were just right exactly.

"St. Nicholas even knows how big we are," said Kat.

"Oh, I wish St. Nicholas Day would last a week," said Kit.

"That reminds me," said Vrouw Vedder, and she looked at the clock. "Half-past ten, and these children still up! Bless my heart, this will never do! Come here, Kit and Kat, and let me undo your buttons!"

"May we take our new clothes to bed
with us?" Kat asked.

"Yes, just this once," said Mother Vedder, "because this is St. Nicholas night."

189

They kissed their Grandfather and Grandmother good-night, and their Mother and Father, and said their prayers like good children; and then they climbed up into their little cupboard bed, and Vrouw Vedder drew the curtains, so they would go to sleep sooner.

"Good-night, dear little Twins," she said.

And so say we.

Trieste Publishing has a massive catalogue of classic book titles. Our aim is to provide readers with the highest quality reproductions of fiction and non-fiction literature that has stood the test of time. The many thousands of books in our collection have been sourced from libraries and private collections around the world.

The titles that Trieste Publishing has chosen to be part of the collection have been scanned to simulate the original. Our readers see the books the same way that their first readers did decades or a hundred or more years ago. Books from that period are often spoiled by imperfections that did not exist in the original. Imperfections could be in the form of blurred text, photographs, or missing pages. It is highly unlikely that this would occur with one of our books. Our extensive quality control ensures that the readers of Trieste Publishing's books will be delighted with their purchase. Our staff has thoroughly reviewed every page of all the books in the collection, repairing, or if necessary, rejecting titles that are not of the highest quality. This process ensures that the reader of one of Trieste Publishing's titles receives a volume that faithfully reproduces the original, and to the maximum degree possible, gives them the experience of owning the original work.

We pride ourselves on not only creating a pathway to an extensive reservoir of books of the finest quality, but also providing value to every one of our readers. Generally, Trieste books are purchased singly - on demand, however they may also be purchased in bulk. Readers interested in bulk purchases are invited to contact us directly to enquire about our tailored bulk rates. Email: customerservice@triestepublishing.com

You May Also Like

Local Taxation and the Rating of Machinery.
A Report on the Rating of Machinery, with All
the Decided Cases Thereon,
from 1783 down to the Present Time, Including
the Short-Hand Writer's Notes of the Special
Case, Arguments, and Judgment

Thos. Fenwick Hedley

ISBN: 9780649638468
Paperback: 248 pages
Dimensions: 6.14 x 0.52 x 9.21 inches
Language: eng

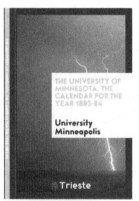

The University of Minnesota. The Calendar for the Year 1883-84

University Minneapolis

ISBN: 9780649057054
Paperback: 140 pages
Dimensions: 6.14 x 0.30 x 9.21 inches
Language: eng

www.triestepublishing.com

You May Also Like

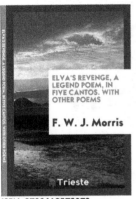

ELva's Revenge, a Legend Poem, in Five Cantos. With Other Poems

F. W. J. Morris

ISBN: 9780649573073
Paperback: 146 pages
Dimensions: 6.14 x 0.31 x 9.21 inches
Language: eng

Neddy Bruce: A Story with Poems. English and Scotch

Adam Smeal

ISBN: 9780649655755
Paperback: 188 pages
Dimensions: 6.14 x 0.40 x 9.21 inches
Language: eng

You May Also Like

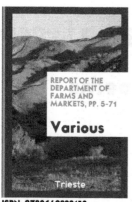

ISBN: 9780649333158
Paperback: 84 pages
Dimensions: 6.14 x 0.17 x 9.21 inches
Language: eng

Report of the Department of Farms and Markets, pp. 5-71

Various

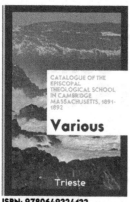

ISBN: 9780649324132
Paperback: 78 pages
Dimensions: 6.14 x 0.16 x 9.21 inches
Language: eng

Catalogue of the Episcopal Theological School in Cambridge Massachusetts, 1891-1892

Various

www.triestepublishing.com

You May Also Like

Three Hundred Tested Recipes

Various

ISBN: 9780649352142
Paperback: 88 pages
Dimensions: 6.14 x 0.18 x 9.21 inches
Language: eng

A Basket of Fragments

Anonymous

ISBN: 9780649419418
Paperback: 108 pages
Dimensions: 6.14 x 0.22 x 9.21 inches
Language: eng

Find more of our titles on our website. We have a selection of thousands of titles that will interest you. Please visit

www.triestepublishing.com